Stars in the Sky

Julie Haydon

Contents

Stars

You can see stars
in the sky at night.
There are lots and lots
of stars.

Stars are very far away.
Stars are like big, hot balls.

Star Colors

Stars can be blue, white, yellow, orange, or red. The color of a star tells you how hot it is.

Blue stars are the hottest stars.

Red stars are
the coolest stars.

The Sun

The sun is a star.
It is a yellow star.

Earth goes around the sun.

We need the sun.
The sun gives us light.
The sun warms Earth.

The sun is much bigger than Earth.
Some stars are bigger than the sun.
Some stars are smaller than the sun.

The sun is the star that is closest to Earth.

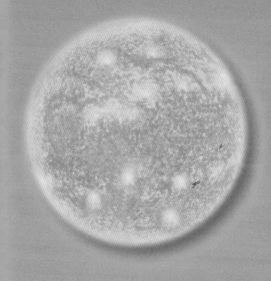

Finding the Way

Long ago, people on ships looked up at the stars. The stars helped them to find their way at night.

Today people can find their way by looking at the stars, too.
But it is hard to see the stars on cloudy nights.

Star Pictures

Some stars make pictures in the sky.

This star picture is called the Lion.

This star picture
is called the Bull.

Telescopes

You cannot see some stars with your eyes.
You need a **telescope** to look at them.

This big telescope can take **photographs** of stars, too.

Glossary

photographs

telescope